Alberta, a young lowland gorilla, finds comfort in the arms of keeper Marcia Mauer. Alberta lives at the San Diego Wild Animal Park, in California.

ZOOS
without cages

by Judith E. Rinard

BOOKS FOR WORLD EXPLORERS
NATIONAL GEOGRAPHIC SOCIETY

Contents

COVER: *Freckles, a llama, gives a friendly kiss to 11-year-old Tracy Stevens at the San Diego Wild Animal Park, in California. "It tickled," says Tracy, who lives in nearby Poway.*

DAVID FALCONER

Escaping the heat of summer, a polar bear sits neck-deep in its pool at the National Zoo, in Washington, D. C. In the wild, polar bears live in icy arctic regions. At zoos, the bears often go swimming to cool off.

NATIONAL GEOGRAPHIC PHOTOGRAPHER JOSEPH H. BAILEY

1
A home for all creatures

Natasha and Nikolai are two young Bengal tigers. They live much as all wild tigers do. They creep through the grass in search of prey. They romp and play together. On hot afternoons, they soak in a shallow pond. At night, they crawl into a safe place to sleep.

The area surrounding the tigers' home looks much like a forest clearing in Asia. But Natasha and Nikolai don't live in an Asian forest. They live in a zoo near Miami, Florida.

Visitors who go to see the tigers can easily imagine they are on safari in Asia instead of at Metrozoo. Grass and tropical plants cover the ground. There are rocks and trees for the cats to climb on. No bars separate the tigers from the people. Instead, a hidden moat surrounds the enclosure. The moat keeps the animals inside and the visitors outside.

"The tigers have a lot of room to move about, and they are healthy and active," says Bill Zeigler, general curator, or superintendent, of animals at Metrozoo. "The tigers chase and pounce on one another in play. That is how we think young tigers train themselves to hunt in the wild. There are things to hide behind in the enclosure, and the tigers spend many hours stalking. They creep up on insects, on birds, and on each other. This is important natural behavior that people couldn't see if the animals lived in cages."

Today, many zoos have a new look. In place of small, cramped cages, designers are building large enclosures that closely resemble the animals' natural homes, or habitats. Parklike enclosures make life better for the animals by providing them with room to behave naturally. The new settings help people understand the animals better by allowing them to see how the animals would really live in the wild.

Leaping high, a Bengal tiger named Natasha romps with her playmate, Nikolai. These tigers live in Metrozoo, near Miami, Florida. Not long ago, some tigers in zoos lived in small, bare cages. Today, many live in open areas much like their native homes.

Early zoos: a changing scene

During a stroll through the London Zoo in 1891, a visitor feeds a cracker to a hippopotamus. In early zoos, keepers knew little about the special diets their animals needed to stay healthy. Often they let visitors feed animals any kind of food. Some foods made the animals sick.

From ancient times, people have enjoyed collecting and displaying wild animals. Long ago, people often worshiped wild animals as gods. In China, monkeys once were considered sacred. They lived in temples and ate from golden plates.

Later, the Romans used wild animals for public entertainment. Bears, lions, and other animals were set loose in arenas to fight each other to the death. Some were forced to duel with armed warriors called gladiators. Many thousands of animals were captured for these violent contests.

For centuries, rulers in many countries collected large numbers of animals such as tigers, giraffes, and peacocks. These animals were kept to entertain royal guests and were symbols of wealth for the people who owned them.

When explorers began to travel to Asia, Africa, and the Americas, they often returned with unusual animals. Kings and wealthy noblemen displayed rare deer and tropical

Big cats, birds, and monkeys crowd a menagerie (say meh-NAJ-uh-ree), or small zoo (left), in Holland. The artist who made this 1751 engraving showed wild animals roaming loose. In reality they probably were locked in cages inside the wire enclosure.

Behind bars, a Bengal tiger named Sam dozes in a pool at the old Crandon Park Zoo, near Miami (below). Built in 1948, Crandon Park Zoo closed in 1980, when Metrozoo opened. Zoos often lack the space to expand their exhibits. Some, like this one, move to new locations.

birds in their private gardens. Eventually, the unusual collections attracted the attention of many people. Small public zoos began to open in many cities throughout the world. The early zoos were called menageries. Most had only a few bears, lions, or tigers. The animals usually paced back and forth inside dark, gloomy cages or in pits.

As interest in wild animals increased, zoos grew in size. It became fashionable for a zoo to try to collect as many species, or kinds, of animals as possible. The animals often lived in cages lined up side by side in large exhibit halls. Keepers allowed—and some even encouraged—visitors to feed the animals.

Large exhibit halls were convenient for visitors. But the halls didn't provide very comfortable homes for the animals. Most keepers knew very little about how to keep the animals healthy. Some animals became sick and died because of disease or poor diet. Others grew restless and bad tempered in the cell-like cages. Sometimes the animals attacked their keepers and had to be destroyed.

Unlocking the cages

In 1907, a man named Carl Hagenbeck opened a new kind of zoo near Hamburg, Germany. It was the first zoo without bars. Open enclosures replaced cages. Animals that usually lived together in the wild shared the same enclosures. The enclosures were landscaped to look like the animals' natural homes. Hagenbeck used moats to separate some of the animal groups. He included artificial rock formations, meadows, and ponds to make the settings seem natural. For the first time, people from cities could see wild animals in a zoo without looking at them through bars.

After Hagenbeck's zoo opened, other zoo designers copied and improved upon his ideas. Now the people who operate zoos are still trying to improve old displays. Many are building roomy and realistic new displays. In wildlife parks around the world, herds of antelopes, zebras, giraffes, and other animals roam large open enclosures. Visitors tour some parks aboard quiet electric trains called monorails. At other parks, people drive their own cars and see the wild animals right outside the windows.

Today, zoos are changing from buildings of metal and brick to areas with open space and naturalistic enclosures. Zoos are changing in other ways, too. They no longer are simply places for entertainment. Now, they are also centers for study and research, places where people seek ways to protect wild animals and to help them live longer and breed as they would in the wild. People who work at zoos know that, for some species, zoos offer the only hope of survival.

At home in a new Metrozoo enclosure, Nikolai prowls near a temple of sculptured stone. The temple resembles one built long ago in a forest

clearing in Southeast Asia. Zoo designers included the temple to make the exhibit more interesting to visitors. Inside are cages where the tigers sleep at night. In the wild, tigers live in the forests of Asia.

9

Monorail glides past grazing herds at the San Diego Wild Animal Park, in southern California (above). In this area, called the Asian Plains exhibit, axis deer, swamp deer, red sheep, and blackbuck antelopes live and raise their young together, just as they would in the wild.

White-tailed gnu (say NEW) gallop across an open field in the San Diego park (right). Once, large herds of white-tailed gnu roamed the plains of South Africa. Hunters killed thousands for meat, hides, and trophies. Now, the animals are found mostly in zoos and in protected areas.

"They're fast!" Michelle and Stephen Risser, 13 and 12, of El Cajon, California, spot gnu from the monorail.

On a wide-ranging tour of the San Diego park, visitors join a truck caravan with park keepers (above). In the Asian Plains exhibit area, keepers Larry Killmar and Nancy Crowe, nearest the cab, watch as riders touch a greater Indian rhinoceros. This rhino knows and trusts the keepers. That's why the keepers allow caravan riders to get close to the animal. Rhinos have poor eyesight and sometimes charge objects they cannot recognize.

In late afternoon, a southern white rhino and her two-month-old calf walk through the South Africa exhibit (right). The rhinos at the San Diego park seem to feel at home. Since 1972, more than forty rhinos have been born in the park.

Curious giraffes wander close to an automobile at Lion Country Safari, in West Palm Beach, Florida (above). Safe inside the car, Holly Guffy and her children watch the animals. Eland (say EE-land), cape buffalo, and zebras graze right beside them. The Guffys live near the park and often drive through. To protect both the people and the animals, all visitors must keep their car windows closed and move slowly. During the tour, Shawna, 13, and Brick, 8, watch lions dozing in the sun. They see elephants, ostriches, camels, and rhinos wandering by. "It's exciting to see the animals so close," says Shawna. "They come right up to the window and look in at you."

13

Making a zoo a home

Ring of water separates zoo visitors from big cats at the National Zoo, in Washington, D. C. (below). A dry moat shaped like a Y keeps the animals in three separate areas. Beneath the grass and trees are animal holding pens, other exhibits, and kitchens.

Pretend you are building a home for your favorite wild animal. How would you go about it? What would you provide for the animal to help keep it healthy and comfortable? What would you add to the new home to make it like the animal's natural home? What kinds of barriers would you build to keep the animal safely inside its home without spoiling your view of it? What would you feed it?

These are some of the things zoo staffs must consider when they plan and build homes for the animals in their care. They must provide many different kinds of homes, because many different kinds of animals live in zoos. The

As his mate stalks nearby, a male lion rests in the sun (right). These lions live in a naturalistic exhibit at the North Carolina Zoo, in Asheboro. A wall of artificial rocks lines the back of the area. Visitors observe the animals from overlooks at the front of the exhibit.

animals come from all parts of the world. Some come from forests, others from deserts. Some are accustomed to warmth, others to ice and snow. Some animals live alone most of the time. Others need to be among their kind in herds, in flocks, or in large family groups.

Laying the groundwork

Before building a home for a particular animal, zoo scientists learn all they can about that animal's natural habitat. Each species is suited, or adapted, to life in a particular environment. Many animals cannot be moved safely from one kind of habitat to another. A polar bear wouldn't be comfortable in a jungle. A lion couldn't get along well in the icy north. Zoos try to provide a setting that matches each animal's habitat as closely as possible. *(Continued on page 18)*

Alarmed by a sudden movement, an ostrich ruffles its feathers and opens its mouth in a silent threat. The movement alerts a giraffe to possible danger (left). These animals share a home with Grant's zebras at the North Carolina Zoo. All three kinds of animals come from Africa. In the wild, animals of these species often share an area.

Its long neck lowered, a giraffe receives an ear inspection from an ostrich (below). The ostrich probably saw the giraffe twitch an ear and came over for a closer look. The keepers say that ostriches are very curious animals.

At the edge of a forest, an African lowland gorilla climbs a slope (left). Five gorillas live in this grassy setting at the Woodland Park Zoo, in Seattle, Washington. Visitors can watch them eating, grooming one another, caring for their young, and building nests.

Gentle giant, a 460-pound (209-kg)* male gorilla pulls on a tree branch (below). Keepers put branches in the exhibit as playthings, so the huge apes won't become bored. The gorillas also nibble on the leaves and bark.

*Metric figures in this book are given in round numbers.

IRA BLOCK

(Continued from page 15)

Before planning a new exhibit, zoo scientists study the habits of each animal. Jumping animals, such as kangaroos, are used to having plenty of room. Mountain sheep and goats usually stay in high, rocky places where they can climb. Burrowing animals, such as badgers and prairie dogs, seek out places where they can dig a home. Bears usually have dens for hiding and pools for cooling off.

Arranging a site

After finding out what an animal needs to be comfortable in a zoo, scientists must decide how to house it. Modern zoos organize and arrange animal exhibits in different ways. Some put similar kinds of animals together. At the National Zoo, in Washington, D. C., lions and tigers share a large exhibit area. The big cats live in outdoor enclosures separated by hidden barriers. This kind of exhibit allows people to compare different species and see how they are alike and how they differ in appearance and in behavior.

Another way zoos arrange exhibits is by grouping together different animals from one large region or from a single continent. At the Bronx Zoo, in New York City, more than two hundred Asian mammals and birds live in a large outdoor park. The park is divided into different exhibit areas. Each area is landscaped to resemble a particular kind of habitat found in Asia. There are forests, meadows, hills, and a river. Animals are placed in the proper habitat. Exhibits like this give people a chance to see many species living together, much as they do in the wild.

Some zoos exhibit animals by grouping together those from one small region or habitat. The Arizona-Sonora Desert Museum, a park near Tucson, contains only animals that live in the Sonoran Desert, which stretches from Mexico into the southwestern United States. The Minnesota Zoo, near the twin cities of Minneapolis and St. Paul, has a wildlife display that includes only animals native to the forests, lakes, streams, and prairies of Minnesota.

Sandy Friedman, assistant director for biological programs at the Minnesota Zoo, reports that the exhibit of local wildlife is very popular. "Our visitors enjoy seeing the wild animals that live around them," he says. "Our zoo is a northern zoo. It is very cold in Minnesota during the winter. The people have to endure the cold weather just as the animals do. So our visitors appreciate seeing how the animals survive in the cold."

Today, when you visit an up-to-date zoo, you see animals feeding and playing, running and jumping, and burrowing underground. You find them splashing in pools, climbing

Crocodiles soak in a tropical rainstorm at the Bronx Zoo, in New York City (below). An artificial storm occurs several times daily. It helps produce the dampness the reptiles are used to in the wild.
At right: a false gavial (say GAY-*vee-ul) floats in the water. This crocodile uses its sharp, pointed teeth to catch fish.*

*Aiming for color, François Caron, 15,
of Aylmer, Quebec, in Canada (above),
focuses on flamingos at the
Metropolitan Toronto Zoo, in Ontario.*

*Flamingo rests on one leg at the San
Diego Zoo (below). The bird may
sleep on one leg, with its head folded
over its back.*

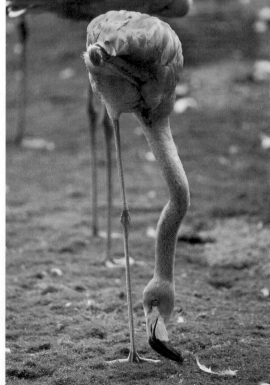

cliffs, swinging through trees, and hiding under rocks. Their homes are as different as the animals are.

Many zoo homes are so carefully designed that they make you feel you are visiting wilderness areas of Asia, Africa, Australia, or North or South America. In many exhibits steep cliffs, boulders, and overhanging rocks form barriers that keep the animals in their enclosures. Many of these formations are made of concrete. They look so natural and blend so well with the landscape that visitors usually think the concrete formations are natural ones. An artificial cave at the Arizona-Sonora Desert Museum looks and feels so real that it fools even scientists. Visiting geologists have asked to chip samples from the walls. They are surprised when attendants tell them that the walls are built of concrete, plaster, and a plastic called polyurethane (say pahl-ee-YUR-uh-thane).

Bringing it all to life

Zoo designers and builders use a variety of display techniques and special effects to create natural-looking habitats for the animals they exhibit. In the reptile house at the Bronx Zoo, a tropical rainstorm strikes several times a day. Lightning flashes, thunder booms, and rain pours down over a steamy jungle swamp. Crocodiles from Southeast Asia and from India hide among jungle plants or climb onto rocks to soak in the downpour. The thunder comes from a tape recording made during a heavy rainstorm. The lightning is produced by bright flashing lights called strobes. The rain comes from overhead sprinklers.

In many modern bird exhibits, such as those at New York City's Bronx Zoo and California's San Diego Zoo, the birds live inside a huge enclosure. Entering the enclosure, visitors experience the sights and sounds of a tropical rain forest. Artificial waterfalls tumble down rocky cliffs among palm and rubber trees, flowering plants, and thick vines. Brightly colored birds of many different kinds live in such exhibits, including hummingbirds, toucans (say TOO-cans), tanagers (say TAN-uh-jers), and parrots.

Some of the birds dart in and out of the waterfalls to bathe. Others perch quietly on branches or flutter through the leaves. They do not seem to be afraid of people. They often fly quite close to the visitors.

No glass panels or wire screens separate the birds from the people. Visitors watch the birds from ramps that extend from the shaded forest floor to the sunlit treetops. In these exhibits, people actually enter the birds' world and walk among many species living together in the same habitat.

Hands cupped, 12-year-old Chrissy Miles, of Portland, Oregon, offers mealworms to a honeycreeper (below). In the walk-through hummingbird exhibit at the San Diego Zoo hummingbirds, honeycreepers, and other species live together. Visitors can stroll close to the birds and watch them dive for insects or hover near flowers to sip the juices. A keeper let Chrissy help out at feeding time. "Most of the birds are so tame they fly right up to you," she says.

Perched on a branch, an aracari (say ah-ruh-SAH-ree) smooths its feathers (left). This aracari lives with other birds of South America in a forest exhibit at the Bronx Zoo.

Tall trees draped with vines and mosses provide hiding places for aracaris (below). These birds use their canoe-shaped beaks to gather fruit.

The world of darkness

Did you know that during the night, while you're asleep, many animals are wide awake? Animals that are active at night are called nocturnal. Normally, you wouldn't be able to see nocturnal animals, such as bats and owls, in action. They rest during the daylight hours. But at the Bronx Zoo you can see them going about their nightly activities.

The zoo has an exhibit called the World of Darkness. There, more than 400 night creatures move about in a dark, shadowy world. Very dim lights make the animals think it is a moonlit night instead of day. But visitors can still see the animals clearly.

In darkened forest settings, the visitors watch as tree snakes, monkeys, and sloths creep and climb among the branches. In a nearby woodland, creatures called sugar gliders move silently through the air. In large, spooky caves, bats flutter and dart about. Frogs and alligator-like reptiles called caimans (say KAY-muns) swim in a dark pool in the cave floor.

At night, after the visitors leave, white lights come on. The animals then go to sleep, just as if it were daytime.

Eyes gleaming, an owl monkey peers into the darkness (above). In the wild, this small animal lives in the forests of South America. At night, its large, sensitive eyes help it hunt for fruit, insects, and birds to eat. During the day, it sleeps in a hollow tree. Owl monkeys are the only nocturnal monkeys in the world.

Startled by a soft noise, a spotted genet (say JEN-net) perks up its big ears (left). Genets have keen hearing and eyesight. These senses help them find rodents, birds, and other small prey in the dark. Ancient Egyptians tamed these catlike animals and kept them in their homes to hunt mice.

Barn owls roost in the World of Darkness building. These owls are expert night hunters. They have such keen hearing that they can pick up even the softest rustling noises made by mice or other small animals.

23

From an overlook, Debra and Susan Morgan watch as a desert bighorn sheep climbs in its enclosure. This sheep lives at the Arizona-Sonora Desert Museum. Here the exhibits copy the surrounding desert and include

Bighorn surveys its home from a rock (above). In the wild, these sheep climb high. This helps them avoid enemies.

native animals and plants. Debra and Susan, 11 and 13, live in nearby Tucson, Arizona.

Crouching motionless and alert, a kit fox listens for sounds of movement. This small fox has an excellent sense of hearing and can move its ears separately in different directions. This helps it avoid enemies and find prey. In the cool of the night, the kit fox searches for kangaroo rats, lizards, and insects to eat. During the hottest part of the day, it sleeps in a burrow, or underground den, that it has dug in the ground.

25

Windows on wildlife

Andrea Osterholt lives in Wayzata, Minnesota. In her home state there are lakes, ponds, and streams, thick forests, open woodlands, and prairies. Many wild animals live in Minnesota: beavers, otters, turtles, moose, lynx, and gray foxes. Andrea is 10 years old. Although she knew about all of these animals, she had not seen many of them until she visited the Minnesota Zoo. In the wild, the animals usually stay hidden. But at the zoo, visitors can see them in their hiding places.

A large area called the Minnesota Wildlife Trail contains more than a hundred animals native to Minnesota. They live in habitats ranging from lake and stream edges to the heart of a northern forest.

"One of my favorite exhibits is the beaver pond," says Andrea. "I like it because you can see all the things that beavers do. You can even see inside their lodge."

In this exhibit, a family of two adult beavers and their four young live in a pond with ducks, turtles, salamanders, muskrats, and fish. Birch and aspen trees surround the pond. A dam forms one end of it. At the edge of the pond is a concrete lodge where the beavers live and raise their young, called kits. In the wild, beavers build their own lodges of mud and branches.

From the edge of the exhibit, visitors watch the activities of the beavers. The animals gnaw through the trunks of small trees and eat tender leaves. They sometimes pile the fallen logs onto the dam. At other times they drag logs into the water and disappear below the surface. Every day, keepers put fresh trees in metal holders around the pond. The beavers may cut as many as twenty trees a day.

"If you walk down a ramp beside the pond, you can see what the beavers do underwater," says Andrea. "There are big windows there. You can look through and watch the beavers swimming around or going in and out of the lodge. Sometimes they pile logs and branches near the lodge entrance. They feed bark to their babies."

The beavers use their teeth to shred the wood of some trees into thin strips. They use the strips to make a soft bed on the floor of the lodge. A TV camera gives visitors a look inside the beavers' home. "The place where the beavers live is above the waterline. It looks really cozy," Andrea says.

In addition to local wild (Continued on page 32)

JIM BRANDENBURG

Window on a watery world lets visitors see beavers at work. The beavers live in a concrete lodge at the Minnesota Zoo, near the twin cities of Minneapolis and St. Paul. They enter and leave the lodge through an entrance below the surface. One beaver strips a meal of bark from a tree (right). Large, webbed feet and a paddle-like tail help the beaver move quickly and easily through the water.

Sights from the sea

N.G.S. PHOTOGRAPHER JOSEPH H. BAILEY

Shana and Nemo, two Atlantic bottlenose dolphins, leap high to touch beach balls (above). These dolphins live at the Brookfield Zoo, near Chicago. They perform many stunts. Their trainers say that when the dolphins learn stunts and perform, they stay healthy, active, and alert.

Close enough to touch, two beluga whales swim near visitors at the Minnesota Zoo (left). Big windows give viewers the feeling that they are in among the whales.

Just beyond a window, a beluga whale peers at Andrea Osterholt, 10, of Wayzata, Minnesota. The belugas seem as curious as the visitors. Often they stare at people as if to ask, "Who's on exhibit—you or me?"

ANNIE GRIFFITHS

*"Hi! Who are you?" A beluga whale
pauses near a visitor at the Minnesota
Zoo. Natives of arctic waters,
belugas communicate with others of
their kind by making a wide range of
sounds. Some of the sounds travel for
many miles through the water. At the
zoo, underwater microphones pick
up the sounds and carry them to the
visitors' area.*

JOHN PERRONE

(*Continued from page 26*) animals, the Minnesota Zoo has animals from other northern regions of the world. Many of those accustomed to snow, such as musk-oxen and Siberian tigers, live outside year round, just as they do in the wild.

The beluga whale exhibit is one of the most popular features at the zoo. "Beluga" comes from a Russian word for white. Belugas are white whales that live in the icy waters of Hudson Bay in Canada and in other northern regions.

At the Minnesota Zoo, the belugas live in a huge tank filled with salt water. Windows line the sides and the bottom of the tank. Visitors can look into the tank from the side, or they can walk beneath the tank and watch a whale glide by above their heads.

When you visit a modern zoo, look carefully. You will experience many new sights and sounds. But there is much happening that you can't see. To find out what else goes on at a zoo, you must go behind the scenes. Let us take you there. You will discover a city at work.

Paddling with its king-size feet, a polar bear swims across a pool at the National Zoo (right). In the wild, polar bears spend much of their time in the icy waters of the Arctic. There they hunt seals, fish, and other sea creatures.

Separated from visitors by a thick pane of glass, a polar bear dives (below). Polar bears use their front legs to pull themselves through the water. They steer with their hind legs.

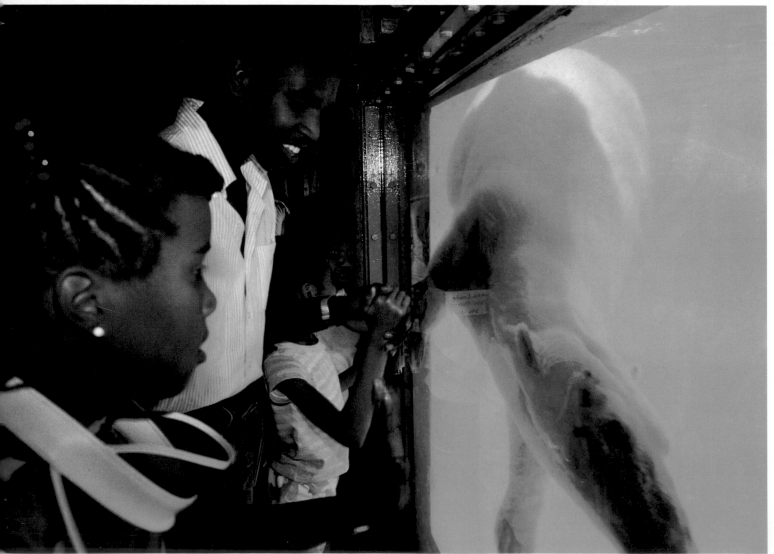

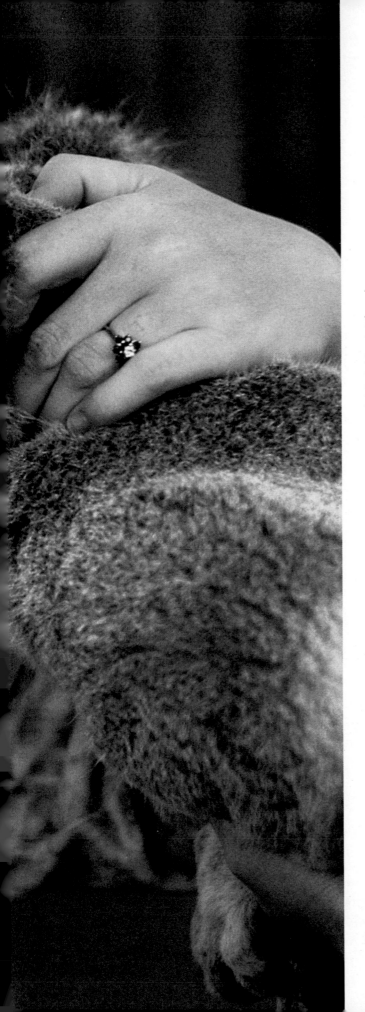

2

The working city

Running a zoo is a big job. It requires the work of many people. In some ways, a zoo is like a city. A zoo has policemen to protect the residents and the visitors. There are gardeners to maintain the grounds and sanitation crews to keep them clean. The zoo director, like a mayor, plans improvements and oversees new projects. There are people who provide food. And there are people who care for the sick and the injured.

Dr. Jane Meier is a veterinarian, an animal doctor, at the San Diego Zoo. She and three other veterinarians take care of more than 3,000 animals that live at the zoo.

The doctors' workday begins at 7:30 in the morning, long before the zoo opens to visitors. "The first thing we do is visit the zoo hospital," says Dr. Meier. "There, we check on animals that are very sick or those that have been injured. We find out if their condition has changed during the night. Then we treat animals that need medicine, bandaging, or other kinds of care."

During a typical day at the hospital, Dr. Meier might treat a parrot with the sniffles, a lizard with a broken leg, a snake with sores on its skin, or a reindeer with an infected foot. After finishing her work at the hospital, Dr. Meier stops to visit the nursery, where many baby animals are cared for. She makes sure that the babies are eating enough and that they are healthy.

With a comforting arm around a koala's neck, San Diego Zoo veterinarian Jane Meier performs an eye examination. Koobor the koala had been squinting, and his eyes had been watering. Dr. Meier discovered that he had an eye infection.

Morning rounds

Each morning, the team of doctors makes rounds of the zoo grounds. "We check the animals in the exhibits," says Dr. Meier. "We want to see if there have been any injuries or illnesses during the night. If an animal has been injured, we treat it before the public arrives. Visitors can upset a patient. Then we have a hard time calming it down again."

How do zoo animals get hurt? "An animal might fall or cut itself on something in its enclosure," Dr. Meier says. "Sometimes animals fight when a new animal is brought into an exhibit. Injuries also occur when visitors throw food into an enclosure," says Dr. Meier. "The animals fight over

DAVID FALCONER

It's 6:30 a.m. at the San Diego Wild Animal Park, and keeper Nancy Crowe begins her day. She loads 50-pound (23-kg) bags of grain pellets onto a truck (left). She will deliver the food to a variety of animals, including zebras, gnu, and rhinos. During her rounds, she will count the animals in her area and look each one over for signs of injury or illness.

Fresh hydroponic grass loaded onto a truck by John Holmes will enrich and add moisture to the diets of animals at the Brookfield Zoo (below). Hydroponic grass is grown in water instead of in soil. It sprouts from barley or oat seeds and grows about six inches (15 cm) in a week.

N.G.S. PHOTOGRAPHER JOSEPH H. BAILEY

the food, and often they seriously hurt one another. Feeding animals the wrong foods can make them sick. So we station guards at the exhibits to try to prevent visitors from feeding the animals."

If an animal has a broken bone or some other serious injury, it may need an operation at the zoo hospital. The vets put the animal to sleep with tranquilizing drugs so they can handle it safely. They use hypodermic needles and darts to inject the drugs. They use heavy gloves, nets, ropes, and portable cages to capture sick animals. "This can be very hard on the animals, but it is necessary," Dr. Meier

explains. "Wild animals don't like being touched. They don't know we're trying to help them. Some can be very dangerous. I've been kicked by several animals and charged by others. But you can't let that interfere with your work. You just have to know how the animals might react, and then protect yourself."

Providing a proper diet

Veterinarians aren't the only people responsible for protecting the health of the animals in a zoo. Other people help, too. One is the nutritionist, or diet expert. Nutritionists work with the vets, the keepers, and the curators to determine the best diet for each kind of animal. The nutritionists prepare animal menus and help order food. Planning the right meals for all the different animals is a big job. The nutritionists must order huge amounts of food to match some animals' appetites. An adult African elephant, for example, eats about 100 pounds (45 kg) of hay a day—and another 25 pounds (11 kg) of grain, fruit, and vegetables. Mary Allen is a nutritionist at the Brookfield Zoo. "It costs a lot of money to feed animals," she says. *(Continued on page 42)*

Fresh fruit and vegetables, dairy products, hydroponic grass, and meat (above) await delivery to animals at the Brookfield Zoo.

". . . and a little extra grain." Mary Allen, a food specialist, discusses an elephant's diet with keeper Don Bloomer (below). She makes sure that the animals at the Brookfield Zoo get all of the foods they need to stay healthy.

"Hey, what's for breakfast?" A curious dolphin watches as a keeper prepares fish at the Brookfield Zoo. A window separates the dolphin tank from the fish kitchen.

Vitamin pill tucked behind the gill of a fish will enrich a dolphin's breakfast at the Brookfield Zoo. Keepers will give this fish to a dolphin during the first feeding of the day. The dolphin is very hungry then, and the keepers can be sure that it will swallow the pill.

Two California sea lions "target," or press their noses against a keeper's outstretched fists at the National Zoo (right). As the sea lions keep still, Lisa Stevens studies their faces and eyes. She looks for signs of illness or injury. After the inspection, she will feed the animals fish from the bucket. Keepers at this zoo train each sea lion to target as soon as it arrives at the zoo. Whenever an animal puts its nose on a keeper's fist, it receives rewards of fish and a lot of praise. The sea lion soon learns to target every time a keeper puts out a fist.

(*Continued from page 38*)   "This year, we expect to spend $327,900 on animal food. We buy a lot of our food from local markets, but some must be shipped from other parts of the country."

The zoo's yearly grocery list includes 75,000 pounds (34,020 kg) of apples, 43,000 pounds (19,505 kg) of bananas, and 42,000 pounds (19,051 kg) of lettuce. The zoo also orders thousands of pounds of hay, grain, birdseed, meat, eggs, and fish. These are the basics. There also are special items such as mice, earthworms, and crickets.

The staff at the Brookfield Zoo buys its food once a week and stores it in a large building called a commissary. Inside, giant refrigerators keep fresh foods from spoiling. The

N.G.S. PHOTOGRAPHER JOSEPH H. BAILEY

"Open wide!" Keeper Tom Huehn feeds a carrot to Perky, a hippo at the Metropolitan Toronto Zoo (above). Giving Perky treats helps the keeper win the animal's trust. As Perky opens her jaws, Huehn has a chance to take a look at the hippo's teeth and gums. Keeping a daily watch on an animal's physical condition is an important part of any zoo keeper's job.

42

commissary opens at 6:30 every morning. Workers there measure out portions of the proper foods for each animal. Then they load the food onto trucks that deliver it to the exhibit areas. At each area, keepers cut up and prepare the foods and feed them to the animals.

Keepers at work

A vet's other partner in keeping animals healthy is the keeper. The keeper knows the animal better than anyone else and can tell by its behavior if it is ill. Don Bloomer, an elephant keeper at the Brookfield Zoo, takes care of two Asian elephants and three African *(Continued on page 47)*

NATHAN BENN (ABOVE AND LEFT)

Hungry crocodiles line up for dinner at the Bronx Zoo (above). As Juan Soto tosses in raw chicken, Bob Brandner keeps the reptiles at a safe distance with the soft end of a broom.

At the sound of a whistle, giraffes head back to the barn at the North Carolina Zoo (left). The animals spend the night indoors where they are safe and where keepers can examine them. Lou Kiessler uses the same kind of whistle sports officials use. The giraffes come when called because to them the sound of the whistle means dinnertime. They eat as soon as they return to their stalls. Keepers at the North Carolina Zoo also call ostriches and zebras with whistles.

Olga the walrus gives a bristly nuzzle to Chris Sammarco, one of her trainers. Nearby, keeper Ed Hausknecht prepares Olga's pool for resurfacing. Visitors to the Brookfield Zoo often see Olga playing with an inner tube. Here, she holds the tube with her back flippers.

N.G.S. PHOTOGRAPHER JOSEPH H. BAILEY

(Continued from page 43) elephants. "The first thing I do in the morning is greet the animals," Bloomer says. "I say 'Good morning' to each one of them. They respond by making rumbling noises. They also spread out their ears. Elephants are intelligent animals. They respond very well. By greeting them each day, I can tell right away what mood they're in and if anything is wrong.

"Next, I clean the animals' enclosure," Bloomer says. "I give the elephants commands to move to one side. Then I clean up all the manure and other wastes that have accumulated during the night. Elephants are big animals, and there's a lot of cleaning up to do. It takes a long time."

Then Bloomer prepares big helpings of hay, grain, fruit, and vegetables for each animal. He feeds the elephants five times a day. Later he will wash them and clean off dead skin. He may trim their toenails and the pads on the bottoms of their feet. In the wild, elephants wear down their toenails and pads by walking over hard ground. At the zoo, the elephants don't move around as much as they would in the wild. Keepers must trim the nails and the pads. Otherwise, they could crack and become infected.

N.G.S. PHOTOGRAPHER JOSEPH H. BAILEY

Keeper-turned-hairdresser, Tom Locke helps a camel molt, or shed, its winter coat (above). Locke works at the Brookfield Zoo.

IRA BLOCK (ABOVE AND OPPOSITE)

Unexpected guest, a baby California mule deer hides at the San Diego park (left). Keepers think the fawn's mother, a wild deer, jumped a fence and moved in because of the plentiful food and the safety inside the park.

Keepers at the San Diego park welcome a new arrival (left). Gerry Bender, right, and Rick Cliffe give shots of vitamins and an antibiotic to a newborn gazelle. They will put an identifying tattoo in the gazelle's ear.

47

Whew! Karen Mosser carries an 80-pound (36-kg) eland toward a field truck. This baby, a male, is only six hours old. Keepers found it during their daily rounds at the East Africa exhibit of the San Diego park. Adult male elands may weigh 1,800 pounds (816 kg).

DAVID FALCONER

Training the elephants is also part of Bloomer's job. The animals learn to stand still, to lie down, and to lift their feet for nail trims—all on command. Commands are very important in helping a zoo vet treat animals. Animals that trust their keepers and obey commands will lie down or stand still while a vet examines them.

Keepers at large outdoor parks, such as the San Diego Wild Animal Park, are called field keepers. Their duties are much like those of city zoo keepers. But field keepers do not work with small numbers of animals in small enclosures. They work with large herds of many different kinds of animals in very large field exhibits.

Every day, field keepers travel by truck through their exhibit areas. A single exhibit may contain more than a hundred acres. Some areas are home to large groups of many different kinds of animals.

Field keepers bring big loads of food and water to all the animals in their area. They count every animal to be sure none is missing. The keepers also observe the herds carefully. They try to spot anything unusual. Such observation requires a keen eye. Wild animals that are sick often do not show it. This is a form of self-preservation. Weak animals become easy targets for enemies.

Carmi Penny is a field supervisor at the San Diego Wild Animal Park. He directs the work of 16 field keepers. "Learning to count and observe so many different animals is hard at first," he says. "But after a lot of training and experience, you develop a skill for it. You look for obvious problems as you drive past a herd of animals. You take a mental picture of the herd. Then, five minutes later, it may dawn on you that something was wrong. Because you know the animals so well, spotting a problem becomes second nature to you." *(Continued on page 52)*

Watched by a giraffe, keepers Mosser and Rick Barongi measure the eland. Later, they will give it vitamins and an antibiotic. After tattooing its ear, they will return it to its mother.

Cleanup time becomes shower time for a Kodiak bear at the Brookfield Zoo (above). Three bears, all brothers, share this exhibit. During the hot summer months, they spend much of their time in the water, keeping cool. The pool often becomes the scene of playful water fights among the bears. Keeper Dennis Grimm, shown here hosing out the exhibit, says that the bears—named Inka, Dinka, and Doo—seem to like playing in the water with an empty keg. They also play with logs. Playthings help keep zoo animals from becoming bored and help provide exercise for them. In the wild, an animal's constant search for food occupies most of its time.

Inka and Doo splash in the cool water of their pool (right). These bears and their brother Dinka were born at the zoo in 1971.

(Continued from page 48)   One of the most important jobs of every field keeper is checking herds for baby animals born during the night. When keepers spot a new baby, they examine it to see if it is healthy. They give the baby vitamins and medicines to protect it from disease. They make a small tattoo in the animal's ear. This helps them keep track of the animal. Then they weigh and measure it to be sure it is not unusually small or weak. They write all of the information in a log. Keeping accurate records for each animal shows which ones are strongest and healthiest. This helps the zoo select animals for future breeding programs.

When accidents occur

Despite all the care keepers give the animals, accidents sometimes happen. When they do, keepers and vets must work together quickly. Often, an animal's life is at stake. Veterinarian Meier remembers one such emergency well: "We found a kangaroo that had stepped into a hole and broken its leg," says Dr. Meier. "The bone was shattered into about twenty pieces. We had to catch the animal quickly, calm it, and take it to the operating room."

Rebuilding the kangaroo's leg bone was a long, complicated process. Dr. Meier and a team of other vets used two metal plates to hold the bone pieces together. Then they put a fiberglass cast on the leg. "The whole operation took us 13 hours," says Dr. Meier, "but we saved the kangaroo!"

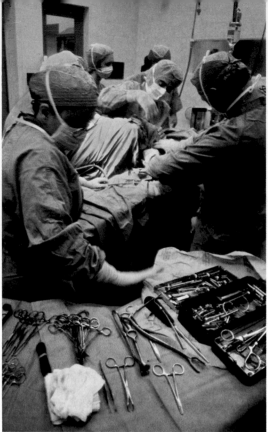

DAVID FALCONER (ABOVE AND BELOW)

Wearing masks, caps, gloves, and surgical gowns, a team of veterinarians and assistants operates on an injured bongo (above). The bongo, an African antelope, pulled its hip out of joint. Dr. Jane Meier, team leader, reaches for an instrument. Other team members give the bongo fluids, hold its leg in position, and watch its heart and breathing rates.

Strong human hands massage the chest of a monitor lizard (left). Other hands pause before pressing a bag that pumps oxygen into its lungs. The lizard's heart stopped after the reptile became chilled. Emergency care at the San Diego Zoo saved the animal's life.

"Now, take a deep breath." Dr. Tom Miller (right) listens to the heart and lungs of a guenon (say guh-NOHN) monkey during a checkup at the Brookfield Zoo.

N.G.S. PHOTOGRAPHER JOSEPH H. BAILEY

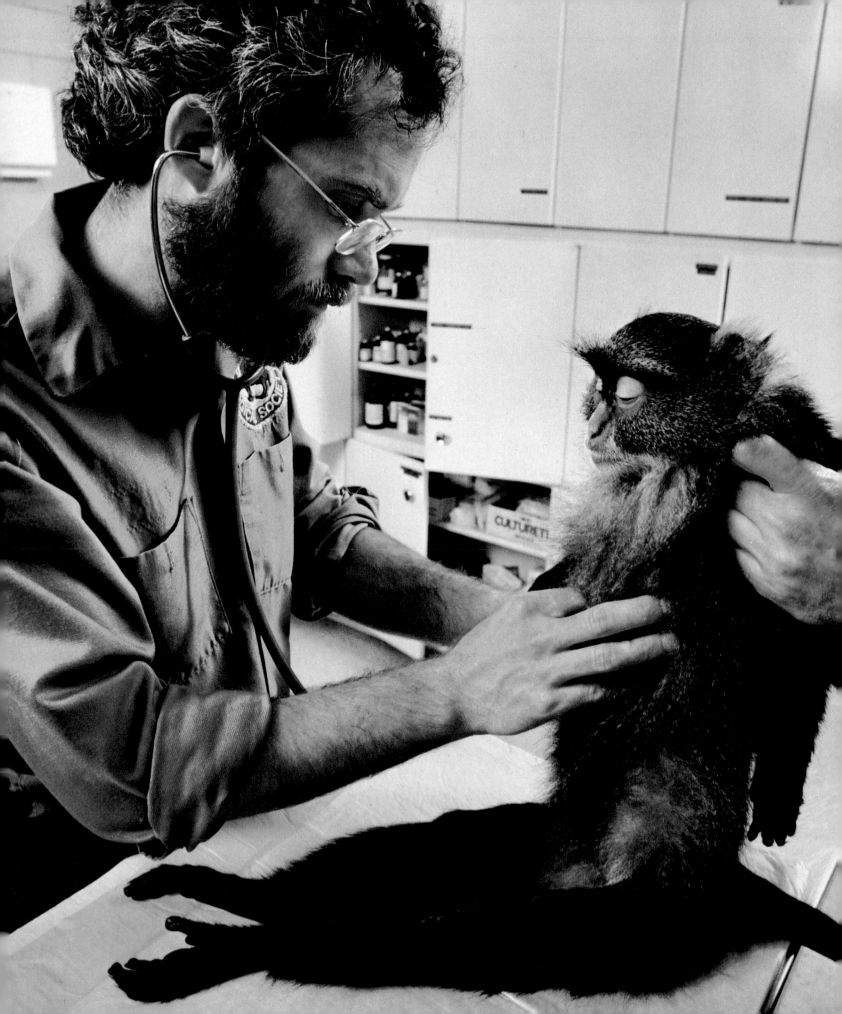

A day in the nursery

The zoo nursery cares for all kinds of young animals. Some are sick, but most simply need care their mothers can't give. Human mothers and fathers provide it instead.

Joann Thomas is a senior nursery attendant at the San Diego Zoo. She and five other attendants act as substitute parents for many kinds of baby animals. "A baby comes to the nursery for one of several reasons," Miss Thomas says. "Sometimes its mother doesn't know how to care for it properly. She may just reject it. Sometimes a mother animal may be sick and unable to care for her young. Or a baby may be too weak to survive without our help."

Substitute parents do everything a mother would do for a child, Miss Thomas says. "We give the babies bottles of formula. We bathe them. We do their laundry if they need diapers. We hold them and play with them."

The zoo nursery often cares for primates—monkeys, chimpanzees, gorillas, and their relatives. "These animals stay in the nursery for about two years because they are completely helpless until that age," says Miss Thomas. "They are almost like human babies. I love all animals, but I especially like working with primates."

The zoo at night

At the end of the day, when the zoo closes to visitors, what happens to the animals? Most of them are taken into barns or other warm places to sleep. Their keepers carefully check them for scratches, cuts, or other problems.

Then night keepers, or guards, take over. A night guard makes rounds of the zoo all night to be sure that the animals are safe and well. A good zoo is not only a busy city—it is also a city that never stops working.

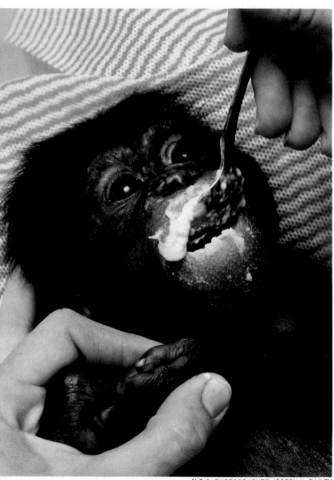

N.G.S. PHOTOGRAPHER JOSEPH H. BAILEY

With its tiny fingers curled into fists, a baby chimpanzee eats mashed bananas from a spoon. Like human infants, baby chimps need constant care. This chimp's mother rejected it. It is being cared for in the nursery at Lion Country Safari, in West Palm Beach, Florida.

As diapered baby orangutans watch hungrily, Joann Thomas gives Lesley, a pygmy chimp, a bottle of milk and water mixed with baby cereal (right). All four babies were born at the San Diego Zoo.

IRA BLOCK

3
To survive and multiply

Just about everyone enjoys watching baby animals. In zoos today, you can see baby animals of many kinds. You might watch a tiger cub romping in the grass. You might spot a newborn giraffe taking its first wobbly steps. Or you might even see a baby bird hatch from an egg right before your eyes.

Try to imagine what it would be like if one day there were no more baby tigers, in zoos or anywhere else. What if all the adult tigers began to die? What if tigers vanished from the earth forever? Without the help of zoos, this could happen—not just to tigers, but to many wild animals.

It's hard to believe that an animal species could disappear forever. But many have. When all the animals of one kind die, that species becomes extinct. Some animals become extinct because they cannot adapt to changes in the environment. Others become extinct because people over-hunt them or destroy their habitats.

Over thousands of years, the number of people in the world has been increasing. As people have spread out over the world, they have needed new land for homes and for growing food. They have cut down forests, taken over grass-lands, and flooded wild areas by building dams. This need for more and more space has destroyed the habitats of many wild animals. When their habitats are destroyed, many wild animals cannot survive. Some (Continued on page 62)

Sachi, a 4-month-old Bengal tiger, plays with a leaf at the San Diego Zoo. Like many wild animals, tigers are in danger of dying out. Educators at the zoo use Sachi and other young animals to teach visitors about endangered species.

IRA BLOCK

Only 36 hours old, a Formosan sika fawn receives a hug—and a belly check—from Penny Kalk (left). "We feel its belly to be sure its mother is feeding it," says Ms. Kalk, a senior keeper at the Bronx Zoo.

Formosan sika stag rubs his antlers against a bush at the Bronx Zoo (right). The stag grows new, soft antlers every spring. By fall they have hardened, and the stag uses them to compete with other stags for the right to mate with females. After mating season ends, the antlers fall off.

In a test of strength, two Père David's stags hold a pushing match at the Bronx Zoo. The stronger male often wins the right to mate with females. A strong father may pass on its strengths to its young.

NATHAN BENN

59

Sun warms the roomy enclosure where Formosan sika deer rest and nibble on plants. Today Formosan sika deer are extinct in the wild. They survive only in zoos and on preserves. About forty live here at the Bronx Zoo. During the day, the deer roam their outdoor enclosure. At night, they stay in shelters, where keepers care for them and feed them grain and hay. The evening meal ensures that they get a balanced diet.

NATHAN BENN

(Continued from page 57) do not survive because they have no place to hide from enemies or to raise their young safely. Others die because they cannot find enough to eat.

Animal groups in danger of becoming extinct are called endangered species. Helping to save endangered animals is one of the most important jobs of zoos today. To protect endangered animals, zoo staffs must give every single one expert care to keep it healthy. That way, the animal can survive and have healthy babies. But caring for animals is not always easy. Sometimes what appears as a simple problem can have serious effects.

A trip to the dentist

Did you know, for example, that animals have dental problems, just as people do? Untreated dental problems can make an animal so sick that it cannot eat or digest its food properly. It may even die.

Janet Fagan, 14, knows a lot about animal dental problems, because she helps treat them. Janet's father, Dr.

Gum disease can be fatal, as an antelope skull shows (below). An arrow points to a place where gum infections destroyed the bone supporting the teeth. The infections, brought on by food decaying between the teeth, helped cause this animal's death. Doctors at the San Diego Zoo regularly treat animals' teeth. The doctors say that good dental care helps many animals live longer and thus produce more young.

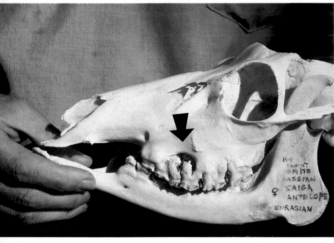

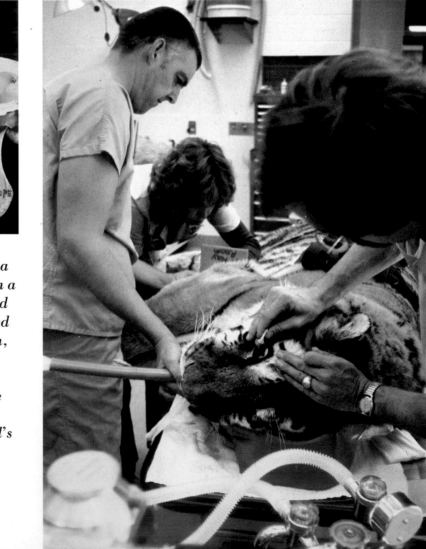

In the hospital of the San Diego Zoo, a surgical team prepares to operate on a Siberian tiger named Ted (right). Ted has several broken teeth and infected gums and jawbone. Dr. David Fagan, left, a dentist, adjusts a tube that directs gas into the tiger's lungs. The gas keeps Ted asleep during the operation. Dr. Philip Ensley, a veterinarian, places a cream on Ted's eyes to keep them from drying out. Terry Willingham, a surgical nurse, connects a tube that will carry medicine into Ted's bloodstream.

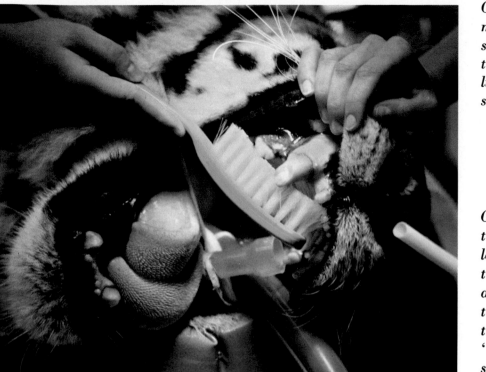

Gentle hands clean food and other material from Ted's teeth before surgery (left). A plastic cylinder holds the tiger's mouth open. As Ted's upper lip is pulled gently back, his teeth are scrubbed with a tiger-size toothbrush.

Operation begun (below), Dr. Ensley, top, inserts a needle to measure the length of a tooth. Then he will fill the tooth. Dr. Fagan, foreground, injects a hard-sealing paste into another tooth. "Before surgery, Ted had trouble eating," Dr. Fagan says. "Afterward, he could chew without showing any soreness at all."

DAVID FALCONER

Watching closely, researcher Suzanne Hansen adjusts the flow of a chemical solution as it drips into a test tube. The solution contains particles that have been separated from the tissue of a zebra. By analyzing these particles, she and Betsy Wedemeyer, right, can determine how closely zebras are related to other members of the horse family. The staff at the San Diego Zoo often makes studies like this one. The information is gathered for use in future projects.

David Fagan, is a dentist at the San Diego Zoo, in California. After school and during vacations, Janet helps her dad perform dental surgery on animals at the zoo hospital and at the zoo's Wild Animal Park. Janet sets up her dad's dental instruments and equipment. She assists in giving animals medicine and helps her father during operations. At the zoo hospital, work may include removing broken teeth from a gorilla, cleaning and filling infected teeth of a lion, performing gum surgery on a tiger, or even filing down the overgrown beak of a parrot.

"It's exciting, it's fun—and it's sometimes a little scary," says Janet. "Once a tiger began to wake up right after surgery. It was a struggle putting it back into its box so the keepers could take it back to the tiger area."

Researcher Arlene Kumamoto checks
a slide before examining it under a
microscope (left). The slide contains
tissue sections from an animal that
died. Zoo researchers carefully study
all animals that die to learn what
caused each death. Scientists want to
know whether an animal died from
disease, from old age, or from some
other cause. They hope to prevent
health problems in other animals.

Improved dental care has helped make many sick animals
healthy again. Scientists in zoos are beginning to design and
build new kinds of equipment and instruments to treat the
teeth of animals. In the future, new dental equipment and
methods will become important aids in saving animals' lives.

Preparing for birth

Zoo scientists are helping to protect animals by studying
their breeding patterns. Some animals do not breed if they
are unhealthy or are in unfamiliar surroundings. Sometimes animals in zoos need space to establish territories,
areas of ground that they defend. Sometimes they need isolated areas to have their young and to raise them. Unless
their needs are met, the animals may not breed successfully.

Polar bears, for example, have mated and had young in
zoos for many years. But the mother bears sometimes killed
their babies. For a long time, zoo experts could not understand why this happened. Scientists studying polar bears in
the wild learned that mother bears need privacy. The bears
always build an isolated den for cubbing, where they have
their young. The mother and cubs stay in the den for several
weeks. When zoos built cubbing dens for their polar bears,
the mothers acted more normally. So many more polar
bears are now being raised in captivity.

Some problems faced by zoo scientists are even more difficult to solve. One problem is learning exactly when animals are ready to mate. Many kinds of animals mate only at
particular times during the year. At other times, males and
females may ignore one another.

Dr. William Lasley is a senior researcher at the San Diego
Zoo. He discovered that by measuring certain substances in

IRA BLOCK

Test tubes filled with urine samples line
a rack in the zoo laboratory. Scientist
Nancy Czekala-Gruber, a specialist in
breeding research, prepares two
samples taken from a female gorilla.
Mrs. Czekala-Gruber is testing the
samples to find out whether the gorilla
is healthy and able to have young.

a sample of urine from some female animals, he could tell when the animals were ready for mating. Other samples told him the approximate time the baby would arrive.

"It's important to know when a baby is to be born," says Dr. Lasley. "Sometimes mother animals do not know how to take care of their babies and may accidentally hurt them. But if you know about when a baby will be born, you can be there to protect it. If necessary, we take the baby from its mother and raise it in the zoo nursery."

Observing in the wild

Helping animals breed in captivity and have healthy young is just part of the work zoo scientists do. They also observe animals living in the wild or in special outdoor research centers to learn more about their behavior.

The National Zoo, in Washington, D. C., has a large research center located in the Virginia countryside. The center is closed to the public. Scientists there observe many kinds of rare species, such as golden lion tamarins, in order to help them survive.

The scientists carefully record the animals' behavior patterns. They want to learn how the animals live together in groups, how they feed, how they raise their young, and how they communicate with each other. This information helps the scientists discover what the animals need to stay healthy. It also helps them build better zoo homes for the animals. A few animals *(Continued on page 71)*

N.G.S. PHOTOGRAPHER JOSEPH H. BAILEY (BELOW, ABOVE, OPPOSITE TOP)

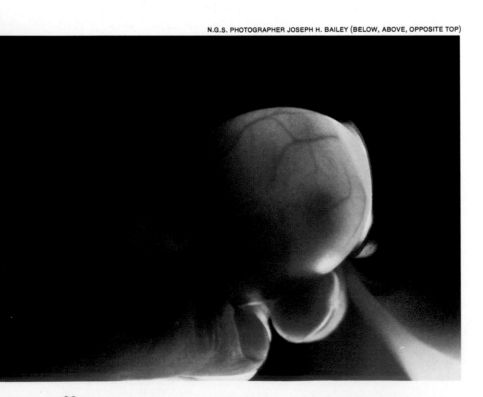

Duck eggs receive a shower at the Minnesota Zoo (above). To hatch, an egg needs warmth and moisture. Normally, the mother's body provides both of these—in just the right amounts. In the zoo, keepers place the eggs in a warming box called an incubator and moisten them by spraying them with water, as Jim Pichner is doing.

Bright light reveals the interior of an egg (left). Keepers check each egg this way two or three times a week until it hatches. "We use the light to watch the development of the chick inside the egg," says Pichner. "That way we tell if everything is going well."

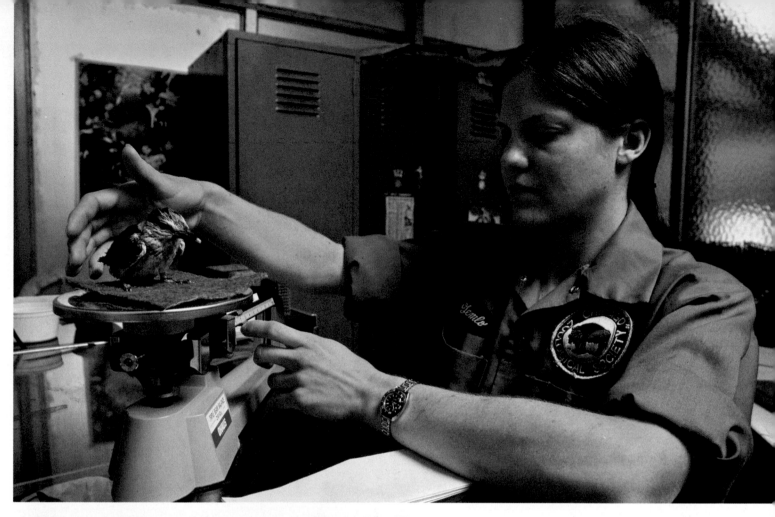

Kingfisher chick balances on a scale in the baby-bird area of the Brookfield Zoo (above). The chick's parents stopped feeding it, so keepers took over. Lucy Gemlo weighs it to be sure it is eating enough. "Baby birds are very fragile," she says. "Until their feathers develop, they are extremely sensitive to cold. We keep them warm in incubators."

In a nursery at the Bronx Zoo, keeper Regina Keenan uses a puppet to give food to a baby Andean condor (left). She does this to make the chick think an adult bird is feeding it. Feeding the chick this way prevents it from learning to depend on humans for food. Zoo officials hope to raise this bird and then release it in the wild. They believe it has a better chance of survival if it does not depend on humans.

67

From the windows of a jeep, a keeper at the Conservation and Research Center of the National Zoo watches a herd of Père David's deer. The center is located in the countryside near Front Royal, Virginia. Scientists there observe many kinds of animals, including several rare species. The scientists hope to learn more about the animals' breeding habits and other behavior patterns.

N.G.S. PHOTOGRAPHER JOSEPH H. BAILEY

(Continued from page 66) in zoos are so rare that even scientists know little about them. To find out more about these animals, scientists study them in their natural habitats. One example of such an animal is the giant panda. In the wild, giant pandas live only in the high mountains of central China. Fewer than twenty live in zoos outside China.

Helping pandas survive

In 1972, the People's Republic of China presented two pandas, a young male and a young female, to the United States. Since then, many thousands of people from all over the nation have come to see the pandas at the National Zoo.

But zoo experts became worried. The pandas grew into healthy adults. Yet they seemed unable to have young. Breeding pandas in captivity has always been difficult.

Zoo experts are now disturbed because the numbers of pandas in the wild seem to be decreasing. Experts estimate that probably fewer than a thousand pandas survive in their native habitat. Since the mid-1970s, many pandas have been found dead. What causes them to die?

To learn more about the problems of giant pandas in the wild, American scientists are working with Chinese scientists in a special program. The program will include the building of a research center near the panda habitat in China. There the scientists will observe pandas both in captivity and in different areas within the habitat. They will attach radio-transmitter collars to some of the animals. Then they will track the pandas as they move through the forests feeding on bamboo, their usual food.

The scientists hope to learn many things from these studies. Some of the questions they will try to answer are these: How many giant pandas are left in the wild? How much space do they need to live? What are their breeding habits? How do changes in their habitat (Continued on page 74)

Working gently, Dr. Devra Kleiman and other scientists at the center near Front Royal open the pouch of a tranquilized wild mother opossum to examine her babies (left). This does not hurt the mother or the young. Opossums live in many areas of North America. They carry their young in pouches, as kangaroos do. The researchers are studying opossums to learn how the babies grow and how long they stay with their mother.

N.G.S. PHOTOGRAPHER JOSEPH H. BAILEY

Releasing the opossum back into the wild, researchers Greg Sanders, left, and Dr. John Seidensticker fasten a collar around its neck (above). The collar holds a small radio transmitter to help them track the animal.

Holding up an antenna, Dr. A. J. T. Johnsingh listens for radio signals from the opossum. The signals tell him where the animal is.

Giant panda peeks through bamboo leaves (left). It is one of two giant pandas at the National Zoo. The pair, a female named Ling-Ling and a male named Hsing-Hsing (say shing-shing), live in their own private compound. The compound is air-conditioned. In the wild, giant pandas live in a mountainous area of China that is usually cool.

Growling a warning, Ling-Ling approaches Hsing-Hsing during a brief spring outing (above). In the wild, pandas are solitary animals. They avoid other pandas for most of the year. Pairs come together only in the spring, during mating season. At the National Zoo, the two pandas are kept in separate enclosures most of the time.

Ling-Ling swats at Hsing-Hsing to keep him off her platform. For several years, scientists hoped that the pandas would mate and have babies. But after eight years at the zoo, the pandas had not mated. Some of the scientists think that such problems may be related to behavior or to diet. They hope to learn more about pandas by studying the animals in the wild.

African Stanley crane begins to puff up its head feathers (left). It may do this to try to scare enemies, say scientists at the center near Front Royal. The enlarged head resembles a cobra—a deadly snake most animals avoid.

N.G.S. PHOTOGRAPHER JOSEPH H. BAILEY (LEFT AND BELOW)

White-naped crane from eastern Asia roams a field near Front Royal. This kind of bird is endangered. Scientists are looking for ways to save it.

(Continued from page 71)   affect the pandas' behavior? How much bamboo does a panda need to eat to stay healthy? What else does it eat in the wild?

Finding answers to the last two questions is particularly important. Since the mid-1970s, large parts of the bamboo forests in the giant panda habitat have flowered and died. Some kinds of bamboo grow for many years. Then suddenly the plants bloom, produce seeds, and die. It may take several years for a new crop to grow from the seeds and again provide a dependable food source. Scientists want to find out how this will affect the giant pandas. They want to set up an emergency plan if the pandas begin to run out of food.

If the scientists learn enough, they may be able to help save the pandas. Perhaps they can help pandas breed in captivity. Such research takes time, money, and cooperation among many people. But for the pandas—and others of the world's wild animals—this kind of research may be the only hope of survival.

Shy monkey called a douc langur (say DUKE LAHNG-gur) holds her year-old baby (right). Fewer and fewer douc langurs survive in their natural habitat in Southeast Asia. The Gladys Porter Zoo, in Brownsville, Texas, lent this female to the San Diego Zoo, which owns two males. The cooperation between the zoos helped to bring about the birth of the baby.

IRA BLOCK

4

The living classroom

"The big, fuzzy tarantula shown here may look scary to some people. But it's not really," says Julie Prchal, 11, of Tucson, Arizona.

"A lot of people think that all tarantulas are vicious creatures that bite and hurt people," she says. "That's not true. Tarantulas that live in the United States are shy. They run away from people. They can't really harm you even if they bite. But they almost never bite unless you frighten them. They eat insects that destroy many plants, so they are helpful to the environment."

Julie has spent a lot of time with tarantulas and other kinds of desert creatures that live near her home. Her father is the assistant curator of small animals at the Arizona-Sonora Desert Museum.

This museum, near Tucson, is an unusual place. It's a zoo—with more than 200 kinds of desert animals. It's a garden—with 550 kinds of desert plants. And it's also a museum—with displays to explain the desert's geology, or natural history as shown in rocks, soil, plants, and animals.

On a clear day, visitors to the museum can see Sonora, a state in Mexico, as well as several mountains in Arizona. They can see cactus plants as tall as trees growing all around the museum. The plants are called saguaros (say suh-WAHR-oze). Saguaros and other desert plants provide food and homes for many different animals.

Some people think a desert is a hot, barren land where nothing can live or grow. But those who visit the museum discover that a desert is really an exciting place filled with living things.

Fierce looking but harmless, a tarantula rests in the hand of Julie Prchal, 11. To most humans, its bite is no more dangerous than a pin prick. Only some species found south of the United States are harmful to people. Julie learned about tarantulas at the Arizona-Sonora Desert Museum, near her home in Tucson.

On a summer field trip, students from Tucson hike into the desert with museum teachers. The students will learn about desert plants, animals, and geology. Teacher Kiki Ochart, right, describes how wind and weather have worn the rocks and smoothed their surfaces.

Discovering the desert

For people like 12-year-old Kenny Kells, of Tucson, the desert museum is a kind of school. One summer, he and several other fifth and sixth graders from Tucson attended classes at the museum to learn about the plants, animals, and geology of their area. Teachers who know all about desert wildlife taught the classes.

"The best part was taking a field trip into the desert outside the museum," says Kenny. "We learned where certain plants grow. We studied the rocks and the minerals. And we looked for animal homes and tracks."

As the class hiked into the desert, they walked single file and stayed close to their teachers. There was hardly a sound and no sign of movement. Yet the teachers cautioned the students to be careful where they stepped and what they touched. All around, the land seemed asleep in the hot sun.

Suddenly, Kiki Ochart, one of the teachers, spotted a big rattlesnake resting in the shade of a rock. Quietly but quickly, he told the class to move away from the area. The snake remained by the rock. When they had moved a safe distance, Ochart stopped to warn the class. "Always be very careful when you walk in the desert," he said. "You may easily surprise a rattler or another venomous animal. They

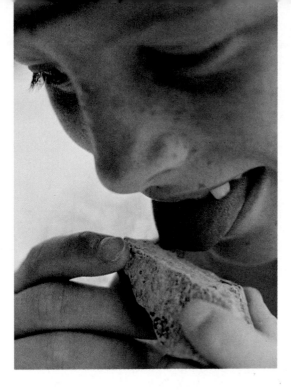

*Tim Ivey, 12, tests a rock sample with his tongue (above) to determine what mineral it is. If particles of the rock stick to his tongue, it is chrysocolla (say cris-so-*KOLL*-uh). If not, the sample is turquoise, another mineral that looks similar. A teacher supervised the test. Many objects are unsafe to taste.*

Peering into a crack in a rock wall (left), the students discover a pack rat's den. "We didn't see the pack rat," says Kenny Kells, 12, wearing the green cap. "But we could see its nest." Small openings in rocks provide safe hiding places and shade for many desert animals.

Shy chuckwalla hides under a log (right). When a predator threatens it, this lizard wedges itself between two rocks and puffs up with air. Then the predator can't easily pull it out.

C. ALLAN MORGAN

usually avoid people, but they will bite if you frighten or startle them. That's why it is important to watch where you are going and to move quietly.

"During the day," Ochart explained as the class continued its hike, "most of the animals stay hidden in cool nests or in underground burrows. At night, when it cools off, they come out to search for food."

Back at the museum, the class saw many of these animals displayed in natural settings. Small rodents, such as pack rats and kangaroo rats, live in artificial burrows inside the museum. During the daylight hours, the animals curl up and sleep in their nests. Visitors can see them by looking through glass panels.

Desert tortoises and lizards live in landscaped outdoor enclosures. The colors of these animals blend so well with the surrounding rocks and plants that it is hard to spot them at first.

"This kind of protective coloring is called camouflage (say KAM-uh-flahj)," Ochart told the class. "It helps an animal hide from predators. The tortoise also has a hard shell to protect it. When a predator attacks, the tortoise pulls in its head and seals the shell openings with its scaly legs."

Fruit of a prickly pear cactus makes a meal for a desert tortoise (below). The tortoise is so well adapted to life in the desert that it can survive for months without drinking water. Its body converts some of the plants it eats into water, which the tortoise stores for long periods of time in bladders inside its body.

"Many plants that desert animals eat can also be eaten by people," says museum teacher Linda Hennessey (right). Here, she serves jelly made from the fruit of the prickly pear cactus, the plant in the foreground, to Jodie Roy, center, and Debra Morgan, both 11. The girls ate the jelly on flat bread made from the beans of mesquite (say mes-SKEET), another desert plant. "The jelly was sticky, gooey, and good!" says Jodie. "I wondered what it would taste like. It was sweet, kind of like watermelon."

C. ALLAN MORGAN

Surviving in the desert

The class learned that desert animals have some unusual ways of surviving in their dry home. Most desert creatures, the students learned, can get by with little water. These animals find most of the moisture they need in the foods they eat—in plant stems, in seeds and fruits, and in insects and other animals.

The class watched how some animals move across the soft sand. They saw a lizard scurry across its sandy exhibit area, then dive out of sight in the sand. The lizard used its wide toes to help it move across the sand and bury itself quickly. Speed and digging ability help some kinds of lizards escape from predators.

A rattlesnake called a sidewinder moved across its enclosure. As the class watched, the snake looped and rolled its body sideways. The sideways motion left a trail across the sand that resembled a series of S's.

In their classes at the museum, the young people not only learned many interesting things about how desert animals live, but they also began to understand that desert plants and animals depend on each other for survival. This delicate balance can easily be disturbed—or even destroyed—by harming even a few plants or animals.

"Remember," Ochart told his students, "the desert is the natural home of these living things. You are only a visitor to their habitat."

Curve-billed thrasher nests in a cholla (say CHOY-yuh*) cactus. The sharp spines of this cactus protect the female bird and her eggs from snakes and other predators. Debra Morgan discovered the bird in a garden at the museum.*

Learning about wildlife

Children at the Minnesota Zoo study sea animals in a shallow saltwater aquarium. Volunteer Betty Anderson shows a class how to touch a delicate sea star without hurting it.

For people who live in cities, a zoo is one of the few places where they can learn firsthand about wild animals. Some are animals the people might never see anywhere else.

The Minnesota Zoo has a saltwater tank where sea creatures, such as sea stars, anemones (say uh-NEM-uh-neze), and sea urchins share an exhibit similar to their natural habitat. These marine animals were collected along the rocky coast of northern California. At the exhibit, students discover how the animals move and feed in the sea. They see how the animals react to each other. They even have a chance to touch some of the creatures during a guided tour.

After touching a ferret, a small weasel-like animal held by Frances Brown, students at the Fort Worth Zoo sniff their hands. They smell a musky odor left by the ferret. The animal marks its hunting territory with musk made by glands in its body.

In an anatomy class at the Fort Worth Zoo, instructor Cleve Lancaster cuts into a rat snake that has died (below). He shows the students the snake's bones and organs and explains how they are constructed and how they work. The students also study birds, mammals, and fish that die at the zoo. The studies help them find out how the animals are alike and how they differ in body structure.

N.G.S. PHOTOGRAPHER JOSEPH H. BAILEY

At the Fort Worth Zoo, in Texas, visiting students listen to the sounds made by screech owls. They examine the rattles from a rattlesnake's tail to learn how the snake makes its warning noise. They also feel the fur, the skin, and the feathers of living animals. They discover that a zebra has a bristly coat; that snakes have cool, smooth scales; and that baby birds have small, soft feathers called down.

Schoolchildren in the greater Los Angeles area can get a closeup look at animals from their city zoo without ever leaving their schools. The Greater Los Angeles Zoo Association delivers birds, reptiles, and mammals to schools aboard a truck-drawn trailer called the Zoomobile. The trailer is carefully set up for the comfort of the animals. It contains roomy cages, a heater, fans, and a large water tank with a hose for easy cleanup. Volunteers from the zoo travel with the Zoomobile. They tell about the animals, answer questions, and set up a petting table where students can touch some of the animals.

Volunteers in action

Excited audience members meet the puppets after a show at the National Zoo. Puppet shows help teach visitors about the problems caused by feeding snacks to the animals.

Officials at the Fort Worth Zoo believe that one of the best ways to learn about animals and their needs is to help care for them. Each year, the zoo invites students to become assistant keepers for a day. The assistants help the keepers prepare the animals' food. They help feed such animals as kangaroos and tortoises. They learn what foods the zoo animals need to stay healthy.

Many visitors like to feed the animals. But the wrong food can make animals sick. Helping people understand why they should not feed the animals has become a problem for zoo officials.

A group of teen-age volunteers spent part of a summer presenting puppet shows for visitors to the National Zoo. The shows explained the dangers of feeding snacks to the animals. Professional puppeteers supplied the puppets and helped the young people prepare the shows. The shows demonstrated that throwing things into an animal's enclosure or trying to tease it can frighten the animal. A frightened animal may hurt itself.

Jacqueline Charles, 14, of Takoma Park, Maryland, helped with the shows. "Some of our puppets looked like animals and some looked like people who visit the zoo," she said. "We also had a big, furry puppet called a Zoodle. Whenever a visitor-puppet did something wrong, the Zoodle would pop up and tell it to stop because it could hurt the animal or make it sick!"

As a volunteer, Jacqueline had a chance to take several tours of the zoo with the keepers. She learned much more than she could have on her own. The zoo also benefited from her help. Without volunteers, many zoos could not offer the variety of programs that they do today.

Behind the scenes, Michelle Cooke, 13, on the left, and Shelley Massey, 15, move puppets during a performance (right). They and 73 other youngsters from the Washington, D. C., area volunteered their time to help the zoo present the shows.

N.G.S. PHOTOGRAPHER JOSEPH H. BAILEY

Art at the zoo

One of the most popular activities for children at many zoos is drawing pictures of the animals and the exhibits. Drawing is fun—and educational, too. It encourages a young artist to observe details. It also helps the artist remember what he or she sees.

At the National Zoo, youngsters draw pictures of some of their favorite animals and then display them in one of the zoo's classrooms. On these pages, you can see some of their drawings.

Craig Hamen, 10, lives in West St. Paul, Minnesota. Last year, he and other members of his third-grade class studied about tropical rain forests. They decorated their classroom to look like a rain forest. Using colored paper, paste, paints, and other materials, they created large trees, vines, tropical flowers, and wild animals.

Then they visited an exhibit at the Minnesota Zoo that resembles a rain forest in Southeast Asia. There, they saw some of the plants and animals that they had made and learned even more about them.

Back at school, they used their new knowledge to make their exhibit more lifelike. "When we were finished our room looked like a jungle," says Craig. "Our parents even came to see it!"

ZOOLAB/NATIONAL ZOOLOGICAL PARK/SMITHSONIAN INSTITUTION (ABOVE AND LOWER LEFT)

Settled down to rest, a lion with a thick mane peers through the grass. Lions spend many hours resting each day.

Giraffe bends down to nibble on a shrub. With its long neck and tongue, a giraffe is able to eat tree leaves that are beyond the reach of most animals.

Artists Craig Hamen and Brennan Sullivan, both 10, put the finishing touches on a painting of a snake (below). Craig, left, and Brennan live in West St. Paul, Minnesota.

ANNIE GRIFFITHS

Hungry elephant munches a twig. It tears off twigs and leaves with its long trunk.

Striped tail makes a red panda resemble a raccoon. This panda is related to the giant pandas of China.

91

Volunteers help at zoos in many ways. Adult volunteers lead tours, teach classes, and do research. Both adults and young people can take part in a program available at some zoos. They can "adopt," or sponsor, an animal in the zoo. People who adopt an animal contribute money to help pay for its feeding and care. The zoo often provides a list of animals available for adoption. The list tells how much it costs to take care of each animal for a year. Then people choose an animal from the list and pay for part, or all, of its expenses for one year.

Conne Dillon helps run the Adopt-an-Animal program at the Sedgwick County Zoo, in Wichita, Kansas. "More than three hundred people help support the animals in our zoo," she says. "Many are children. The children seem to enjoy helping the animals by giving money for their care. Classes often sell candy, wash cars, or raise money for their animals in other ways."

One third-grade class at Wells Elementary School, in Wichita, decided to adopt a baby squirrel monkey, says Mrs. Dillon. The class sold birdseed to raise the $30 necessary to care for the animal for a year.

As sponsors, the students received a certificate from the zoo thanking them for their help. Then a zoo keeper talked to them and told them all about the squirrel monkey.

"Because the children worked so hard to raise the money, we asked them to name our baby squirrel monkey," says Mrs. Dillon. "They named it Swinger."

The class is looking forward to visiting the baby monkey often and watching it grow up. Your class may want to adopt an animal, too. Visit or write your *(Continued on page 98)*

Playful hippos push each other during a swim. They live at the Sedgwick County Zoo, in Wichita, Kansas. Hippos can stay underwater for several minutes. The Sedgwick County Zoo has a glass-walled hippo pool where people can see the animals underwater.

NATHAN BENN

With a loud squawk, a Blue-fronted
Amazon parrot seems to be saying hello
to Gretchen Gragg, 16, of Wichita
(left). The parrot lives in a large jungle
habitat at the Sedgwick County Zoo.
Educators there take visitors through
the display to watch the tropical birds
flying, nesting in the trees, and eating
fruit. Many youngsters enjoy watching
the parrots. With their strong beaks,
the parrots crack open seeds. They
use their feet both for climbing and for
picking up fruit to eat.

NATHAN BENN

"Look up there!" Zoo curator Barbara
Burgan points out a bird in the
treetops of the jungle exhibit (above).
The exhibit has a thick growth of fruit
trees, including banana, lemon,
papaya, and pomegranate.

Fluffing its feathers, a Lilac-crowned
Amazon parrot gets a cool shower at its
home in the Sedgwick County Zoo.
During hot weather, keepers often
spray the birds with water.

Enjoying the show

(Continued from page 92) local zoo to find out if it has such a program. If you do decide to visit the zoo, don't miss the animal shows. At some zoos dolphins, seals, elephants, and other animals perform for visitors every day. The animals are trained to do stunts that demonstrate their physical abilities and their intelligence.

Gary Miller, an elephant trainer at the San Diego Wild Animal Park, says that training elephants in captivity is a very important part of keeping the elephants healthy. "Elephants are intelligent animals," he says. "If they don't have

Keeper Tom Huehn gives an elephant a friendly pat at the Metropolitan Toronto Zoo (left). Keepers often take time to tell visitors about their animals and to answer questions.

At the San Diego Wild Animal Park, an elephant named Nita performs tricks. First, she lies over her trainer...

...then she helps him up. Here, Nita uses her trunk to lift trainer Gary Miller to his feet.

new things to learn, they quickly become bored. This makes them less active and less alert. Then they are more likely to get unruly, or possibly sick. Training and performing every day gives them plenty of mental and physical exercise."

The elephants stand on their hind legs, hop on three legs, sit, kneel, and pick up objects with their trunks—all on command. Many of these activities are not really tricks. They are things that elephants do naturally in the wild.

Have you ever wondered what it would be like to ride an elephant yourself? At some zoos you can find out. The

Bronx Zoo offers elephant and camel rides to young visitors during the summer. The animals are trained to carry passengers gently around a large, round track.

Eleven-year-old Wanda Wright, of New York City, decided to ride a camel at the zoo. "At first, I was frightened of the idea," she says. "But when I saw how much fun the other people were having, I made up my mind to try it. When it was my turn to get up on the camel, it felt like I was being lifted high in the sky. I sat on her hump. Her hair felt soft, and the ride was very smooth. It was so smooth that I didn't want to get off at the end."

Preserving our heritage

Touching, or even riding, a wild animal is only one highlight of a visit to a modern zoo. Today zoos offer a variety of things to see and to do, to feel and to smell, to hear and to read, to discover and to understand.

Zoos today are better places than ever before for both animals and people. Zoo scientists, builders, keepers, and veterinarians all work hard to give the animals the best care and provide them with the best homes possible. Zoo educators and volunteers try to help people understand the animals better.

In the past, people did not always care about the wild animals of the world. But things are changing. More and more, zoos are showing that people can help wild animals—and by doing so, make their own lives richer.

What a way to travel! Douglas Freeman, 7, and Wanda Wright, 11, both of New York City, enjoy a ride on a gently swaying camel at the Bronx Zoo. Camels live in the deserts of Africa and Asia and are a major means of transportation. Camels can go for several days without food or water.

Probably extinct in the wild, the Mongolian wild horse survives in zoos. This female lives in a small herd at the Bronx Zoo. These horses were once plentiful in Asia. Gradually, they died out because of overhunting and loss of their habitat to domestic cattle.

NATHAN BENN

Index

Bold type refers to illustrations; regular type refers to text.

At dusk, a giraffe nibbles hay and leaves that hang from a tree at the San Diego Wild Animal Park.

DAVID FALCONER

Additional Reading

Readers may want to check the National Geographic Index in a school or public library for related articles and to refer to the following books: Buchenholz, Bruce. *Doctor in the Zoo* (Viking, 1974). Caras, Roger. *Going to the Zoo With Roger Caras* (Harcourt, 1973). Caras, Roger. *Zoo in Your Room* (Harcourt, 1975). Hewett, Joan. *Watching Them Grow: Inside a Zoo Nursery* (Little, Brown, 1979). Perry, John. *Zoos* (Franklin Watts, 1971). Scott, Jack Denton. *City of Birds and Beasts: Behind the Scenes at the Bronx Zoo* (G. P. Putnam's Sons, 1978). Shuttlesworth, Dorothy E. *Zoos in the Making* (Dutton, 1977). Time-Life. *Life in Zoos & Preserves* (Time-Life Films, Inc., 1978).

Consultants

Sue Pressman, The Humane Society of the United States; Robert O. Wagner, American Association of Zoological Parks and Aquariums, *Chief Consultants* Dr. Glenn O. Blough, Judith Hobart, *Educational Consultants* Dr. Nicholas J. Long, *Consulting Psychologist*

The Special Publications and School Services Division is grateful to the individuals, organizations, and agencies named or quoted within the text and to the individuals cited here for their generous assistance: *Arizona-Sonora Desert Museum:* Christopher L. Helms, Janice Hunter; *Chicago Zoological Park (Brookfield Zoo):* Joyce Gardella; *Fort Worth Zoological Park:* Cleve W. C. Lancaster; *Friends of the National Zoo:* Pat Petrella; *Garlough Elementary School, West St. Paul, Minnesota:* Ann Hansen; *Greater Los Angeles Zoo Association:* Kaye Jamison; *Lion Country Safari, Inc.:* Susan R. Cox, Leon Unterhalter; *Metropolitan Toronto Zoo:* Mary-Ruth MacQuarrie; *Miami Metrozoo:* T. A. Strawser, R. L. Yokel, Bill Zeigler; *Minnesota Zoological Garden:* Sandy Friedman, Nancy E. Gibson, Ron Johnson; *National Zoological Park:* Ilene Ackerman, Dr. Robert J. Hoage, Dr. Devra G. Kleiman, Dr. Dale L. Marcellini, Michael Morgan, Patricia Powell, Dr. John Seidensticker, Dr. Christen M. Wemmer, Judith White, William A. Xanten; *New York Zoological Park (Bronx Zoo):* John L. Behler, Dr. Donald F. Bruning, William G. Conway, Mark C. MacNamara, Joan Van Haasteren; *North Carolina Zoological Park:* Marcia H. Constantino; *San Diego Wild Animal Park:* Martha Baker, Carmi G. Penny, Suzanne M. Strassburger; *San Diego Zoological Park:* Georgeanne Irvine, Kathy Marmack, Dr. Arthur C. Risser, Jr.; *Sedgwick County Zoo:* Mark C. Reed; *Smithsonian Institution:* Dr. Thomas R. Soderstrom; *Woodland Park Zoological Gardens:* Laurence Gledhill, David Hancocks; *World Wildlife Fund—U. S.:* Lynne Lehman.

Far-out Fun: Barbara Gibson (1, 6, 10, 12-13, 16); Roz Schanzer (2, 3, 7, 11, 14-15); Drayton Hawkins, N.G.S. staff (4-5); Arthur Iddings (8-9); Lois Sloan (poster art and dry transfer art).

Composition for *Zoos without cages* by National Geographic's Photographic Services, Carl M. Schrader, Chief; Lawrence F. Ludwig, Assistant Chief. Printed and bound by Holladay-Tyler Printing Corp., Rockville, Md. Color separations by the Beck Engraving Company, Philadelphia, Pa.; the Lanman Companies, Washington, D. C.; Lincoln Graphics, Inc., Cherry Hill, N.J.; National Bickford Foremost, Inc., Providence, R.I. *Far-out Fun* dry transfers produced by Dennison Manufacturing Co., Framingham, Mass.; wall poster printed by Intelligencer Printing Co., Lancaster, Pa.

Library of Congress CIP Data

Rinard, Judith E.
    Zoos without cages.

    (Books for world explorers)
    Bibliography: p.
    Includes index.
    SUMMARY: Discusses the concept of open zoos, introduces some zoo workers, and describes some activities happening in zoos today. Includes a poster and a booklet of games and puzzles.
    1. Open-air zoos—Juvenile literature. 2. Open-air zoos—United States—Juvenile literature. [1. Open-air zoos. 2. Zoological gardens] I. Title. II. Series.

QL76.R56   590'.74'4   79-3243
ISBN 0-87044-335-6 (regular binding)
ISBN 0-87044-340-2 (library binding)   AACR2

ZOOS without cages

by Judith E. Rinard

PUBLISHED BY
THE NATIONAL GEOGRAPHIC SOCIETY
WASHINGTON, D. C.

Gilbert M. Grosvenor, *President*
Melvin M. Payne, *Chairman of the Board*
Owen R. Anderson, *Executive Vice President*
Robert L. Breeden, *Vice President,
Publications and Educational Media*

PREPARED BY THE SPECIAL PUBLICATIONS
AND SCHOOL SERVICES DIVISION

Donald J. Crump, *Director*
Philip B. Silcott, *Associate Director*
William L. Allen, William R. Gray, *Assistant Directors*

Staff for Books for WORLD Explorers Series: Ralph Gray, *Editor*; Pat Robbins, *Managing Editor*; Ursula Perrin Vosseler, *Art Director*

Staff for Zoos without cages:
    Margaret McKelway, *Managing Editor*
    John Agnone, *Picture Editor*
    Drayton Hawkins, *Designer*
    Louise Ponsford, *Assistant Designer*; Catherine O'Neill, *Picture Legends (Chapter 2)*; Mona A. Enquist, Pat Rosenborg, *Researchers*

Far-out Fun and Supplementary Activities: Patricia N. Holland, *Project Editor*; Ross Bankson, Jane R. McGoldrick, *Text Editors*

Engraving, Printing, and Product Manufacture: Robert W. Messer, *Manager*; George V. White, *Production Manager*; David V. Showers, *Production Project Manager*; Mark R. Dunlevy, Richard A. McClure, Raja D. Murshed, Christine A. Roberts, Gregory Storer, *Assistant Production Managers*; Susan M. Oehler, *Production Staff Assistant*

Staff Assistants: Debra A. Antonini, Nancy F. Berry, Pamela A. Black, Barbara Bricks, Nettie Burke, Jane H. Buxton, Mary Elizabeth Davis, Claire M. Doig, Rosamund Garner, Victoria D. Garrett, Nancy J. Harvey, Joan Hurst, Suzanne J. Jacobson, Artemis S. Lampathakis, Virginia A. McCoy, Merrick P. Murdock, Cleo Petroff, Victoria I. Piscopo, Jane F. Ray, Carol A. Rocheleau, Katheryn M. Slocum, Jenny Takacs, Phyllis C. Watt

Intern: Andrea V. Borden

Market Research: Joe Fowler, Carrla L. Holmes, Meg McElligott, Stephen F. Moss, Marjorie E. Smith, Susan D. Snell

Index: Sarah K. Werkheiser